MY DAY OF INFAMY

MY DAY OF INFAMY

LINDA S. FRITZ

XULON ELITE

Xulon Press Elite
555 Winderley Pl, Suite 225
Maitland, FL 32751
407.339.4217
www.xulonpress.com

Paperback ISBN-13: 978-1-66288-874-8
Ebook ISBN-13: 978-1-66288-875-5

MONDAY SEPTEMBER 10, 1973

**the date my world was hit with
the worst tragedy of my life!**

**A tragedy that would haunt me for the
next 49 years, and beyond.**

Dedicated to my son, Josh Wesley Fritz

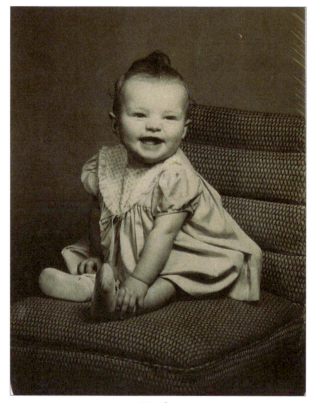

Linda

I was born Sunday, October 03, 1948, at 10:25 A.M. in Fort Worth, Texas, at Harris Memorial Methodist Hospital the daughter of Dolly Mae (Cunningham) Stokes and William Ray Stokes. I was one of over 40 babies born that day. Doctor J W. Hewatt was the doctor and Irene was the nurse. I weighed in at seven pounds and thirteen and a half ounces with a height of nineteen and three-fourths inches.

I would live in Fort Worth, Texas, until I was almost four years old, when my parents and their friends moved back to Kentucky. Here, in Kentucky, I would live the rest of my life.

Linda, Dad, Mom

I was surrounded with both sets of loving grandparents, Atta Clio (Smith) and Hubert Ray Stokes, my paternal grandparents, and Robbie (Bridges) and George Clyde Cunningham, my maternal grandparents. In addition, I was blessed with both sets of great grandparents, my paternal great grandparents, Mary Hannah Lucinda Elizabeth (Keith) and Henry Jackson Stokes. My maternal great grandparents were Lena (Guier) and Drew Bridges.

1

Linda with Baby Doll

Like all little girls, I loved my dolls. I played with them, changed their clothes, carried them with me when Mother and I went shopping or when we visited my grandparents. However, before I turned four years old, my Bonnie Braids 'Vinylite' plastic head doll became sticky from the heat. (Later it was learned this type of plastic seeped a mysterious sticky substance.) Mother was concerned with Bonnie Braids sticky face and took the opportunity to burn her in the trash barrel while I was taking my afternoon nap.

However, I had a dream of my mother burning Bonnie Braids. I jumped out of my bed and went running through the house to the backdoor and into the backyard screaming, "Do not burn Bonnie Braids. Do not burn my doll!" She knew how much I loved this doll and I presented a hard time for her to confiscate my Bonnie Braids doll from me. Therefore, she took the only opportunity to send "Bonnie Braids" to Doll Heaven while I slept!

But there would be many more dreams, haunting dreams in my life.

Linda in front, Mava, Judy.

At the age of nine years old, I accepted Jesus Christ as my Lord and Savior. I had been to church on a particular night with my maternal grandparents, Clyde and Robbie Cunningham at Maple Grove Baptist Church in Trigg County, Kentucky. I was spending the week with them. We three girls, Judy and Mava (Fuzzy) Cunningham and I were spending this particular night at Judy's house. I loved staying and visiting with Judy and her family. Judy's mother and dad, Josephine and Hershell Cunningham, were my favorite aunt and uncle in all Trigg County, I totally loved these two people. Anyway, while we were in bed giggling and talking, I made the statement I wanted Jesus to come into my heart. The three of us prayed. I prayed really hard and sincerely.

I personally asked Jesus to come into my heart and be my Savior. OH! WOW! Did Jesus come into my heart! Today, I can still feel the emotional rush and tinkling feeling when the Holy Spirit entered into my heart. A feeling one does not ever wish to forget, and thankful you do not ever forget.

Also, while I was in the third grade, I began having dreams about people we knew, of family members and acquaintances that would pass away, would die. I never shared with anyone anything about these dreams. As a child, I would feel guilty when they passed away, because I felt I had somehow caused their death. These dreams would continue all way into middle school, and it was at this time I felt I could no longer handle whatever was going on with these dreams.

Linda on Silver

We were at my grandfather's farm this particular day and I had just finished riding Silver. I combed him, fed him a treat, and then turned him loose into the horse lot. I was still thinking about the dreams and decided to talk to God. I walked over to one of the barns and then walked around to the back so no one could see me and began talking to my Heavenly Father. I told Him I did not understand the meaning of the dreams, nor why I was chosen to have the dreams. I finally just simply asked that He take away the dreams. He did, but a few years later certain feelings would come over me before certain bad things happened. My grandmother had had certain dreams throughout her life, as did my mother. Howard and I loved the breakfast table each morning, just to hear what Mother dreamt the night before.

One dream my grandmother dreamt was during World War II. I was in high school when she shared this dream with the family. Her second son, Albert Dale Cunningham, was drafted at the age of eighteen. Along with other boys from Trigg County, he loaded the bus for Blanding Boot Camp in Florida, and then onward to active duty in Europe. Grandmother woke up in the wee hours of this particular morning and told Granddaddy that Albert was dead. Grandmother had dreamt of Albert holding his arm out, the arm that was shot, calling to her. She in turn was holding her arm out and telling Albert, "Come on. Come on Albert." He replied, "I can't Mom, I can't." Their fingers almost touched but then drifted away. At that moment, she knew her son had died there in Southern France. The telegram from the US Army would not arrive until about a month later.

I would share the story about my dreams several years after Bill and I had married and we had been blessed with Josh. The three of us had stopped by my parent's house late one afternoon while they were eating. I related the stories about my childhood dreams causing my parents to stop eating. They stared at each other for a moment. Then Mother stated, "Well! That explains everything." To which I asked, "Explains what?" Daddy stated, "Linda, we could not take you to any funerals when you were young. You would become so upset and we had no idea why. So therefore, we would not take you to any funerals, but leave you with our friends and neighbors."

Linda in 4th grade

When I was in the fourth grade, I began to dream about when I grow up, and there were two things I wanted. The first one was to become an educator, and the second one was to have a little boy with dark hair and dark eyes. I would have dreams about this little boy for years and years and this little boy in my dreams had a face, and his face never changed in any of my dreams.

I experienced a true incident about real temptation and Satan when I was ten years old. One particular Sunday morning when we lived in Russellville, Kentucky, I was walking from Peveler Drive onto 9th Street toward South Main Street. I was headed to the Russellville United Methodist Temple to attend church services with my friends. I soon approached the large two-story white mansion that gracefully stood behind three tall, huge, beautiful trees. The trees were pointing upward to the morning sky protecting the graceful mansion from the heat of the sun.

As I passed the first tree, Satan, yes, Satan, literally jumped out from behind the tree. He commenced to tell me why I should turn around and go back home. No, he did not have a pitchfork, nor was he wearing a red suit! And there were no horns protruding from his head. Actually, he was rather somewhat handsome, and spoke in a soft calm voice. I stopped in my tracks staring into his handsome face.

Daddy had taught me to persevere, and I continued my walk onward toward the Russellville United Methodist Temple. At the third tree, he stepped from behind this tree. He continued to tell me how horrible it would be for me to continue, because no one would know me, and I would be highly embarrassed, etc. I then remembered a Bible story I had read and heard about in Sunday School. Therefore, I looked him in the eye, yes, I was shaking. I boldly stated "Get thee behind me in the name of Jesus Christ!" Poof! He was gone! I then continued my journey onward to the Russellville United Methodist Temple located on South Main before one reached the town square. I do wish I had known at that time that I could have sent Satan to the Abyss!

The front doors were heavy, but I was able to draw enough strength to open them. I stepped inside and witnessed all the people standing and singing. A very kind lady immediately saw me and came toward me. She said, "Honey, the children have already gone to the back. Let me lead you to them." And off we went to the back to join my friends and the other children. Hallelujah!

On our Florida vacation before I entered the fifth grade, I had a near death experience, an experience that still is as vivid in my memory today as that beautiful warm and sunny day. Again, we were staying at the Clearview Motel at Laguna Beach in Panama City, Florida. The motel was in a 'U' shape with the office located facing the street. When you entered the front door to the office, one could view the ocean through the huge window that looked out at the pool and then onward pass the palm trees toward the beach and the Gulf of Mexico. The rooms jetted outward on each side of the office toward the beach, completing the unique 'U' shape motel. When one left their room, there was the pool in front of your door with the invitation for you to come play and swim. And, Daddy was in the office talking to the Hollis's, the owners.

Howard, Mother, and I had gathered the beach bag and float to spend the morning at the beach with the family we had met from Alabama. A lovely family consisting of Karin, who was my age, nine years old, her brother who was three years old like Howard, and of course her mother and father. They were also staying at Clearview Motel where they vacationed each year like us.

The day began with excitement and anticipation for another beautiful, memorable day in Florida. The sun was bright and sending down hot rays with the anticipation of being another perfect day on the beach. The roar of the Gulf waves resonated, not only across the shoreline and beach, but traveled onward up toward the motel. One could only envision the splash of the waves against your body as they rolled in onto the shore. We gathered our floats and towels as we all headed to the beach for a morning of total enjoyment and bliss.

The six of us (Karin, her mother and brother, my mother, brother and me) were floating on our floats laughing, talking, and splashing. We were truly enjoying the waves and the warm sunlight rays against our bodies. There was and had been a sandbar all week just a few feet from the shoreline across the front of the motel. The sandbar created a perfect calm swimming pool from the shoreline to the sandbar to play and feel safe. We had enjoyed the safety of the sandbar which provided a great area to swim and play in the waves.

Mother needed to go to the room, so she left while the rest of us rode the waves on the floats. Later, Karin and I decided we did not want to float anymore. Therefore, her mother was going to take Howard and her brother to the beach to watch us and let the boys play in the sand.

Now, let me insert, there was a young gentleman who had checked into the Clearview Motel very early this particular morning to get some rest. Daddy was in the office talking to the Hollis's. We had become very close friends with the Hollis' by staying with them over the years each summer. However, while Daddy was socializing with the Hollis's, he witnessed the young man coming out from his room with a cup of coffee. Then, he immediately threw the cup of coffee toward the pool and began running toward the beach where he had heard the screams of "Help! Help!" Daddy knew there was a crisis at the beach. He also knew his family were the ones on the beach. At that moment, Daddy took off at full speed.

When I jumped off the float, I gave the float Howard was on a huge shove toward the beach for the waves to carry him to shore safely, and I jumped off into a "whirlpool." Unknowingly, we had floated away from the safety of the sandbar! Karin jumped off her float doing the same.

They say your life flashes before you when you die, and I had also heard that you get three chances before going down into the water before totally drowning. I can remember when I went under the first time to stay calm and I tried. I had been taught some water safety tricks at my swimming lessons when a person is in trouble in deep water. As I was going under, I looked up and I could still see and feel the sun rays penetrating through the water. I was able to force myself up and take another huge breath before going under a second time. Yes, I called on Jesus, my Savior! I then thought, He is here helping me to the surface of the water again! I felt a calmness and peace over taking me as I slipped under the water the third time, for I had and was totally prepared to meet my Jesus. This time I felt the water dragging me further and further under into the depths. However, this time I felt a hand grabbing me and lifting me up and out of the abyss into the air and then over into my Daddy's arms. There are truly no words to totally express how my Daddy's arms felt around me. I clung to him as he did me for what seemed like eternity. I was beyond a safe feeling now, I was in a total secure feeling of safety, because my Daddy's arms engulfed me.

Then, the thought arose within me, I can only imagine the feeling of one day having Jesus' arms around me when I meet him in Heaven!

Let me say, to this day that this experience instilled within me a true feeling of more respect for the waters of the Gulf of Mexico, in addition to the Atlantic Ocean, the Pacific Ocean, or any body of water.

Not a time following this experience would I ever sit on the beach in Florida and not relive this near-death experience I had before entering into the fifth grade. For even today, while sitting on the sandy beach in Destin, Florida, along with Daddy Bill, this near-death experience of how I had almost died in the waters of the Gulf of Mexico surfaces in my memories. After surviving the whirlpool, as I grew older, I realized just how precious each day is that God gives us and how quickly a life can be taken.

We have no idea who the young man was, for he had stopped in the wee early morning hours of that day to rent a room and rest. He came out of the room at the right time to hear the screams from a frightened mother and to save two young girls from meeting their Creator, one from the state of Kentucky, and one from the state of Alabama.

Daddy tried to find him after all the commotion from the whirlpool, to thank him, but to only discover that he had checked out following the incident. Mother would later say, "He was an angel sent from Heaven to save Karin and me. Yes, over the years since that day, I have totally believed he was an angel sent from God to save two young girls. He, (God) had many things left for me to accomplish on my journey on earth before going home to Heaven.

Let me insert here about an incident that occurred one night between my Freshman and Sophomore year. I woke up during the night, which is highly unusual for me being a super sound sleeper, to discover an angel, or one could say an apparition, standing at the foot of my bed. I was not afraid. I sat up in the bed to gaze upon this beautiful and serene apparition standing at the foot of my bed. No words were spoken, for I only felt a sense of peace and calmness. I cannot truly say how long we gazed at one another. However, again, I can say, I felt only warmth, calmness, and a sense of peace. Today, when I feel apprehension or turmoil in my life, the vision of this angelic angel enters my memory. I guess maybe, in a way, she is a guardian angel.

JOSH WESLEY FRITZ

Bill and Linda's Photo for Adoption Agency

Bill and I had been married seven years when we decided to start a family. All of our friends had children, and we witnessed the joy of a family with children. So, we began praying to God, our Heavenly Father, for a family. However, we felt God was speaking to us about adopting a child. We prayed about 'adoption' and felt the voice of God speaking to us to adopt a child, for there were so, so many children in need of a home. And, we felt that we had a lot to offer a child.

Therefore, we contacted the local Christian County Children's Services and submitted our papers for the adoption of a little boy. In just a few weeks, we were contacted by the Christian County Children's Services. The agency felt they had a match for our personalities. We met with the social worker to discuss this little boy. Needless to say, Bill and I were elated about this little boy.

We returned home to pray, for we wanted to make the correct decision. We were about to make the most important decision in our lives. This decision was going to affect three people's lives. Bill and I prayed hard in order to know what God's direction for us was in this situation. Like I said, three lives were at stake here, mind, Bill's, and one little boy's whole life.

Bill

I began decorating one of the extra bedrooms into a little boy's room, a room for our little boy, our son. We purchased a baby bed that was white with red and blue stars at the ends. I had our friends, who own an upholstery shop, to recover my toy box with the stagecoach on the front with blue leatherette material. I also painted my toddler furniture that Mother had saved all of these years white. I got a friend to cut out wooden stars that I painted red and blue to be attached behind the painted knobs on the drawers of the chest, and also attached stars on the knobs of the chifforobe. I then hired a seamstress to make drapes with patriotic soldiers to hang at the windows and I then finished the room off with a sculpture deep red carpet. Now, the wait began.

Linda sitting on the toy box in Josh's room

I purchased a Wonder rocking horse that had a spring-suspension and was manufactured to never turn over, as well as to last. The cadmium plated springs were guaranteed not to stretch or break, as well as support 200 lbs. The horse I purchased was named Cheyenne, a Palomino which made me think of Dixie my Palomino horse I rode and showed. This Cheyenne came with a carved-in lariat and sculptured western saddle and stirrups. Little did I know just how many generations of our 'boys' would ride Cheyenne.

Well, it did not take long for the correct answer to be given to us. We called Christian County Children's Services for an appointment, and the appointment came quickly. We met with the Social Worker to learn the whole story of this little boy, who was soon to become our son. But when she handed me the picture of this little boy, I could only stare at the face of this precious little boy. I stared so long, she became highly concerned and asked me, "Do you know this little boy?" I answered,

"No, but Yes!" I then explained to her that this little boy had been in my dreams since I was in the fourth grade, for I had seen his face in all of those dreams. She seemed to understand and began the arrangements for us to meet and spend time with the little boy.

It is hard to find the correct words to describe how Bill and I felt when we left knowing we were about to meet OUR little boy. Our little boy who had been sent to us from God.

Josh riding Wonder Horse Cheyenne

In just a couple of days, Bill and I drove to the house where he was living with a wonderful foster family, and met with 'Our Son.' We spent most the day with him out in the yard playing, as well as inside the house. The time limit seemed to pass so quickly before we had to leave, and it was so hard for us to leave without him. However, we would return the next day to pick him up and take him HOME. The date was June 7, 1973.

Josh was born September 2, 1971, at 1:10 p.m. He weighted seven pounds and fourteen ounces and was twenty inches long. And! He had brown hair and brown eyes. The little boy in my dreams for so long! My Little Boy!

The Social Worker was at the foster home when we arrived, and everything was in order for us to leave with our son, 'Josh Wesley Fritz.' We joyfully placed Josh in our car, waved good-bye, and backed out of the driveway.

When we arrived home at 3311 Southgate, Josh walked into the house like he had walked into the house his whole life. He seemed to sense, this is my home, and my parents. He walked into each room of the house opening all cabinets, doors, and drawers. In the den, he opened doors and drawers of the end tables and coffee table. He checked out the utility room before walking into the kitchen. Here, he opened each cabinet door to look inside, without ever touching or taking anything. He then traveled to the living room looking around and opening the coat closet door and searching what was in the drawer of the coffee table. He then traveled toward the guest bedroom, where again he opened closet doors and drawers of the end table, chest, and dresser. He continued down the hallway toward the hall bath opening doors and drawers to look inside. He traveled onward to our bedroom and bathroom, again looking in drawers and behind the doors. His final stop was in his bedroom and there he found his toy box. He began playing. For he was 'HOME' at Last!

When I would put Josh in his bed at night, I would sit on the floor beside his baby bed until he was asleep. He would hold onto one of my fingers through the slats until he fell asleep. He usually had his bottle in his mouth, which I would remove when he was asleep. When I thought he was asleep, I would ease my finger loose from his grip. And if he was not asleep, then he would open one eye and look at me and smile. Josh would sleep on his stomach with his knees under him pushing his rear-end upward and with his feet crossed. This made a darling picture of Josh. For he was "My Bundle of Joy From Heaven!" Thank You LORD!

Josh at Great Grandparents Stokes's house

June, 1973, was Josh's first family trip. We loaded our beach ware, cooler with drinks and sandwich meat and headed to the Pennyrile State Park. We also traveled with our nephew Todd, Bill's Mom and sister Sue, and Aunt Ruth. Josh loved playing in the sand, as well as splashing in the water. The same body of water that earned me a 4-H canoeing badge when I was in middle school.

Bill and I headed up the Indian Missions at our church, Bethel Baptist Church in Fairview, Kentucky, and had been collecting clothes for the Navajo Indians for the past year. We had made arrangements to carry all the clothes to the Navajo Reservation in Cuba, New Mexico. Therefore, on July 14, 1973, the three of us loaded up all the clothes into a huge U-haul and the back of the truck. We then headed toward

Cuba, New Mexico, and then onward to Titian Baptist Mission located on the Navajo Reservation.

What a wonderful trip! Bill and I had traveled the pass seven years just the two of us, but now, the three of us would be traveling together. I felt we were now a complete family. I was married to my soul-mate and I was given the little boy of my dreams since I was nine years old. Thank you, Lord! Life is so good!

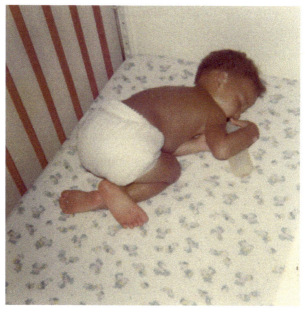

Josh sleeping, notice his crossed feet

When we reached Tinian Baptist Mission Church in New Mexico, located on the Navajo Reservation, Josh and I disembarked from the truck. Bill looked for a spot to park the truck and the U-Haul. I walked on inside Tinian Mission carrying Josh on my hip. I walked through the sanctuary toward the Fellowship Hall, and here I stopped right inside to wait for Bill. At the far left of the Fellowship Hall in the kitchen area stood several ladies with a church group from Louisiana. They were there for one week, also. I just nodded as they did to show recognition.

When Bill entered the Fellowship Hall, we walked toward the ladies and Bill began to introduce ourselves. When I said hello, the ladies laughed and stated, "You are not Navajo. We thought you were." I replied, "No, I am from Kentucky. I guess you thought this was my little papoose?" Let me say, it is fair for them to think we were Navajo because of my long jet- black hair. Plus, both Josh and I had a very good summer tan. (I would learn many years later when I finally did the DNA test that I do have Navajo blood!)

The three of us spent a whole week at Tinian Baptist Mission Church. At night, we slept in the back of the truck. We had packed bedding for this purpose, because we knew there were no motels on the reservation. I thoroughly enjoyed helping the Louisiana Church with Vacation Bible School for the children. I was in my teacher's mode, and was thoroughly enjoying each moment.

Bill, Josh, and I toured the reservation with David Mackenzie, who was the head of the Indian Mission at Tinian Baptist Mission Church. I think one of the highlights of the week was the nightly church services. Here, we met many of the residents who lived on the Navajo Reservation and was able to be a part of the church services.

I did learn to sing the chorus of "When the Roll Is Called Up Yonder" in Navajo. The Navajo language is a very difficult language. I understand how the 'Windtalkers' of WW11 won the war for America. They were a code talker employed by the USA military to use their language as a secret communication. The Navajo language was little known and used at that time.

David had shared with us the story of one widow man with several children who had lost both feet from frostbite. The man raised sheep for a living. One particular cold winter, his feet had gotten frost-bite from attending to his sheep. One night of the revival, the gentleman entered the mission with his bandaged feet using crutches. His beautiful children proudly walked behind him. The scene brought tears to my eyes, while breaking my heart. However, this scenario made me feel pleasing that we had brought all of the clothes to these people. And, I then thought of a young girl who would be warm this winter in my camel Chesterfield coat that my mother had sewn for me when I was in high school.

The day before we were to leave, we helped David move his household items to a new home located in Cuba, New Mexico. Again, our presence was a blessing from God, for we had the U-Haul and the back of the truck to make the move easier and faster. God is Great, and All the Time!

Cuba, New Mexico is a village with a very small population located along U.S. Route 550. It does have a few motels and restaurants. The Fritz family had eaten in one of these restaurants before driving onto the road that led to the Tinian Baptist Mission Church. And it was here located in a small subdivision, we helped the MacKenzie family move.

Let me insert about Josh and Donovan, two little brown babies playing on the reservation. Well, of course, Josh belonged to Bill and me, and Donovan was the son of David MacKenzie and his wife. All week long these two little 'papooses' played around the mission and on the reservation.

Now, Josh was born September 2, 1971, and Donovan was born September 3, 1971, making only one day difference in their age. I joyfully enjoyed watching these two young toddlers becoming friends. They shared their toys and their laughter with each other. And, these two 'papooses' had a wonderful time getting to know each other during our week on the reservation. The thought arose within me, 'Why can't all people in America get along and share one's culture and enjoy one another, just like these two little toddlers.

The day we left, along with the church group from Louisiana, was a sad moment, but a joyous time also. David's mother-in-law, who lived with the family, entered the Fellowship Hall with turquoise necklaces and bracelets on her arm to sell.

Now, I was standing at the far end of the Fellowship Hall, but my eagle eye was on a certain turquoise necklace that immediately caused me to start walking to the far end of the hall. However, by the time I reached the jewelry, my necklace had been purchased by the Louisiana Church Youth Director.

However, a few moments later I saw him with a different necklace and David's mother-in-law with 'my' necklace. I strolled over to asked the Youth Director if he had decided not to purchase the necklace. He replied, "No." He had decided upon a different necklace for his wife. So! I marched over to David's mother-in-law, and purchased 'the' turquoise necklace.

I asked how much the necklace costed, and she replied what her price was for the beautiful turquoise necklace. I promptly paid her that price. However, the Youth Director from Louisiana who was standing beside me, stated, "Wait a minute! You charged me a lot more for that necklace!" She looked up at him and smiled as she nodded and stated, "Yes, you man, and she woman." Needless to say, my lights went on, for I knew at that moment that I needed to purchase all Navajo jewelry from the Navajo ladies, NOT Bill.

(Oh, I did begin to ask the young people what they had paid for the necklaces and the bracelets they had purchased for their mothers. Correct. The boys had paid more than the girls.)

When we returned home from New Mexico, Bethel Baptist Church gave Josh a baby shower. What a shower it was, for Josh received so many toys, wonderful clothes, and story books. One of my favorite items was a red knit tee shirt with his name, JOSH, printed on the back. Josh's son Destin, and grandson Wesley, would one day wear this same shirt. And, there is a picture with each one wearing this same red JOSH shirt.

Linda, Josh, David McKenzie
Tinian Mission in New Mexico

Let me tell an incident that occurred when Josh was almost two years old in our back yard on Southgate. Josh was playing in the sandbox that Bill had built for him and I was soaking up the sun rays lying on the lounge on the patio. Suddenly, I heard Josh whimper. I raised my head to find a huge long black and colored mark snake with his head raised staring at me and my son standing behind him. I know my heart stopped beating, or at the least skipped a couple of beats. I knew not to panic, because the snake was between me and my baby! Still staring at the snake with our eyes locked on each other, I softly told Josh to walk over to the fence, a fence that separated our yard from the neighbors. When he reached the fence, I then softly said for him to walk to the end of the fence and then close to the house and onto the patio. The snake and I still had our eyes locked on one another. When Josh had reached the patio, I instructed him to stand still. I then set my plan in motion.

In my head, I went over what I was going to do one more time and then I quickly jumped up off of the lounge, grabbed Josh, slid the patio door open to run inside. Safely inside, I turned to see the location of the snake who was then slivering toward Hedge, Bill's bird dog. I mentally told Hedge: Kill Him, Pulverize Him! The snake slivered back to Hedge's dog pen. And Hedge threw a complete Bird-Dog Fit arousing all the canines in the neighborhood.

Josh playing in his sandbox

I had been planning for Josh's 2-year-old birthday party after we arrived from New Mexico. The party was held Saturday September 1, 1973 at 1:00 p.m. in the backyard of our house. Josh weighted in at 30 pound and 36 inches in height.

The birthday party theme was animals, with harmonicas and pin paddle balls as party favors. I chose 'Animals' as the theme because Josh could name every animal from a hippopotamus to a Bob White. Okay, I know a Bob White is a bird, but he also knew his birds. The attendees played the game 'Drop the Handkerchief.' However, the most memorable part of the party was when Brock Johnson, a friend up the street who adorned Josh Fritz, poured a dump truck full of sand from the sandbox on top of Josh's head as he walked through the backyard gate and left the party for his home. What excitement this caused! Oh! I had to take Josh inside the house and give him a bath before returning back to HIS birthday party.

Everyone had a wonderful time eating cake and ice cream, playing games in the backyard, and opening presents without any idea what would happen within the next nine days.

Monday September 10, 1973
My date of Infamy,
the date my world was hit with the worst tragedy of my life!
A tragedy that would haunt me for the next 49 years, and beyond.

Okay, here I go with the true story that has been suppressed until now. For you see, every time one drop of memory from this Date of Infamy would enter into my thoughts and memory, I would totally suppress and push it way down within my whole being. The suppression of that day, Monday September 10, 1973, would totally control my being until I finally shared part of the story that had occurred.

No one knows, nor can one even begin to imagine what can happen in their life from day to day, much less within a nine-day period of time.

The year 1973 started off being one of the best years of our seven-year marriage. I was still teaching in the sixth grade at Pembroke Elementary School, it was my second year. We had moved into the 'new' Pembroke Elementary School located on Hwy 115 at the edge of Pembroke, Kentucky. And, Bill and I had our Bundle of Joy. We had traveled to the Navajo Reservation, we had celebrated our son's two-year-old birthday, and I was finishing my master's degree program.

The week after Josh's two-year-old birthday, he came running to me while I was in the back of the house wanting to know who that man was. What Man? I picked him up and carried him toward the kitchen. I carefully looked inside every room of the house on the way to the kitchen. When we entered into the kitchen, I asked Josh where the man was. His little eyes looked around the kitchen and den, and then he pointed to the utility room. I placed him on one of the bar stools and whispered, "You sit right here for me." I cautiously walked over to the utility door and slowly opened it. There was no one there. I knew deep down inside that no one could be inside the house, because from the time that Bill and I had married, he always made me lock all the doors while he was at work or away.

Early afternoon, Josh again asked me who that man was in the living room. Again, I picked him up and cautiously walked toward the living room. Again, there was no man. Josh would again ask this same question the following day.

A couple of days later, Mother and Grandmother stopped to visit Josh and me. They had come to town for some shopping and both wanted to see Josh before going home. As we sat talking and watching Josh playing with some toys, I told them about Josh seeing a man in the house several times. Grandmother smiled and simply said, "He is seeing Angels, Linda." Yes! Angels.

Following my graduation from Austin Peay State University, where I received my teaching degree, I enrolled at Murray State University in Murray, Kentucky, in order to work on my master's degree. Monday night, September 10, 1973, I had class at the University of Kentucky at the Hopkinsville University campus. I was so elated when Murray State University began to offer night classes off campus, making it a relief from driving to Murray each night after school for class. They also offered the reading class I needed to complete my master's degree. On this night, the class was to review for an upcoming test. It was the most important test in order for me to receive the credit needed to finish my master's degree course in education. However, I was about to experience a season of infamy. A day of infamy that I had never experienced in my whole life, and hope I never will again.

The Webster Dictionary defines the word in-fa-my as the state of being well known for some bad quality or deed: such as 'a day that will live in infamy,'

Monday, September 10, 1973, was a beautiful, warm, and sunny day when I awoke. I had a strange feeling from the moment I woke up and got out of bed. I looked inside Josh's room as I walked down the hallway toward the kitchen. He was still sound asleep in his baby bed. Bill had already left for work at the State Farm Office located on Fort Campbell Boulevard in Hopkinsville, Kentucky.

There seemed to be a strange, thick-like atmosphere in the house, an atmosphere I had never experienced at any time in my life. It was like a thin-thick fog, but not a fog that hindered one from clearly seeing through; it was just a strange atmosphere that's so hard to explain or even to describe. The house seemed much quieter than usual, not even the ticking of a clock could be heard nor a bird chirping at any of the windows. It made me question if I was in a dream, but I knew I was wide awake and not in any dream. I began to feel a presence, a very familiar presence, one I had felt before. I thought of the angelic angel who stood at the end of my bed between my freshman and sophomore year. I also thought of Great Granddaddy Jackson, because Mammy always told me that he was watching me from Heaven throughout my life. Or, was it an angel sent by God watching over us?

As I entered the kitchen, everything seemed to be at a standstill. Nothing seemed to be "alive." A total quietness engulfed the kitchen and the den; everything almost seemed like a dream-like atmosphere, and I wondered if I was in the twilight zone. I opened the patio curtains in order to view the patio and the backyard. Hedge, Bill's faithful hunting dog, was strangely quieter than normal. The whole yard just seemed to have no life at all; it looked just like a still-life picture or painting.

I started having thoughts of skipping my night class. This was a feeling I had never had before. I had never skipped class anytime during my school years, at any time or school level. However, the urge to skip class would surface throughout the whole day, and I would just push the feeling away.

Josh's 2 year old birthday party

Josh awoke shortly after I had made some coffee. I retrieved him from his bed and carried him to the kitchen. I put him in his highchair as I fixed his breakfast. I sat down at the kitchen table beside him and together we ate our breakfast with many smiles, and making faces at one another. After we had finished eating, I cleaned the kitchen and prepared for the two of us to go outside to play. Josh loved to play outside in his sandbox and wading pool. And I loved to watch him.

Josh and I spent most of the morning outside playing in the back yard in his sandbox and playing with his toys on the patio. He would laugh and giggle each time he jumped in his wading pool. Oh, such joyful laughter each time he looked at me and splashed the water. However, we both stayed close together, whether we were in the sandbox, in the wading pool, or on the patio. We both seemed to cling closer and closer together all day. A closeness that totally thrills a mother!

Close to noon, we went inside to eat lunch. Again, the two of us sat at the table smiling, laughing and making faces at each other. After lunch, Josh got out of his highchair and brought some toys from his room to the kitchen to play while I cleaned the kitchen. Even at nap time, Josh wanted to sleep in my lap instead of his bed. I was elated that he wanted to sit in my lap and sleep. So, the two of us curled up in the big rocking chair while he took a nap. We both seemed to just hug each other closer that day.

As the day progressed, the feeling of not attending class became even stronger. Again, I would push the feeling away, for I needed to attend class for preparation in order to take the big main test to earn credit for the reading course. And, I just never skipped class, any class, and why was I having the feeling of skipping at this point in my life. The feeling just did not make any sense to me. For here I was coming to the end of earning my master's degree and I am having a feeling to skip class!

As five o'clock rolled around, I began to prepare to attend my night class. Bill arrived home close to 5:30 and prepared to mow the backyard. Josh went with Bill outside to the back yard to play with the neighbors two children. Tammy and Tracey loved playing with Josh anytime they had the opportunity, and Josh loved playing with the two of them. So, here was an opportunity for the three to play.

I finished getting ready and preparing for class. As I walked past the patio door, the feeling of skipping became even stronger. I do not know how long I paced passing the patio door to the carport door; to only turn around and pace back toward the patio door. Each time I passed and looked out the patio door, I would see Josh standing in the back-yard. He would wave at me and throw a kiss, and I would reciprocate.

Each time I passed the patio door, I would walk to the carport door to leave, but I could not turn the door knob to exit. I would hear a voice saying, 'do not go, do not go to class.' I would then turn around and go back to the patio door. I do not remember how many times I paced from the patio door to the carport door. The voice would just keep reso-nating in my mind. At one point, I did make it from the carport door to my car door. But again, I would turn around to go back inside to return to the patio door. This time, Josh was sitting in his wooden chair inside his wagon with Tammy and Tracey pulling him. He waved when he saw me, and of course I waved back and said, 'I Love You!'

Again, I walked back to the carport door, turned the door knob, and exited down the steps onto the carport. This time, I stood at the bottom of the steps looking at my car door. I slowly walked over to the car, opened the door, and got inside my car. I sat there for a few moments telling myself that I needed to get to class. I drove out of the carport onto Southgate. Then, I drove the car onto Virginia Street heading to class at the University Kentucky Campus on the other side of town.

When I arrived at class, everyone had already arrived and was sitting at their desk. Ruth stated as I sat down at my desk, "I thought you might not be attending class, for you are always one of the first ones to arrive at class."

I just smiled, as she kept talking about her day and this reading class. I was about to share with her about the feeling I had had not to attend class when the teacher called the class to order. He was about to call the class roll when Dr. Riley appeared at our class door. We all turned around as Dr. Riley softly stated, "I need to see Linda."

I got out of my seat and started walking toward the door, but as I walked past Ruth's desk, he said, "Bring your books and purse." I returned to my desk and retrieved my purse and class books. A total silence had now covered the class room as I walked to the door. I looked at Dr. Riley and then realized that Henry, our neighbor, was leaning up against the hall wall beside the door, and without any shoes on his feet. I then gazed into his eyes and asked the question, "Is it Josh or is it Bill?"

All Hell had broken loose on Southgate when Bill screamed for Henry!

When our Neighbors had heard the screams from our backyard, and witnessed Henry running from next door to our backyard, they immediately became aware of the tragedy that had occurred in the Fritz's backyard. They began placing phone calls to Jennie Stuart Hospital to report the accident, and to report that Bill and Henry were on their way to the hospital with Josh.

Hurriedly, Henry drove Bill and Josh to Jennie Stuart Hospital. Henry would later report to me how Bill was hugging onto Josh in the car and repeating all the way to the hospital, "I have killed him, I have killed him." "How am I ever going to tell Linda?"

To this very day, I do not remember, nor do I know what route we took to Jennie Stuart Memorial Hospital in Hopkinsville, Kentucky, that night. On the way, I asked Henry, "How bad is it?" His quivering words were, "I do not know!" I then remembered that Bill had just sharpened the blades on the lawn mower! Then, we both traveled the rest of the way to the hospital in total silence.

Looking back, I do believe when I asked Henry how serious was the accident, and he stated that he did not know, was the moment that I entered into the rim of being in 'Total Shock.' My doctor would state later to me that I was in shock. Shock! I had never been told that I was in shock at any time, nor during any crises in my life. But then, how could I have endured what the next days, weeks, and months were going to be like and be able to survive this 'Living Hell' that was before us, if not in shock, total shock.

Henry pulled up to the emergency entrance door of the hospital, and I focused on the sign 'Emergency Door' as I jumped out, and began running as fast as I could. I ran through the doors in search of my husband and baby. When I ran inside the emergency room, a nurse walked up to meet me. She asked if she could help me. I said I am looking for my son. She stated, "He is already in surgery, Honey. Let me take you to your husband." And I began to cry, no, I began to sob!

She and I entered the elevator and began that agonizing long journey up to the second floor, the Surgical Floor! She stated that when they brought Josh into the emergency room, that was the first time since early morning they had had a room vacant to accommodate him. She furthered stated, that was the first time since early morning that the doctor was free to perform surgery. So, when they arrived with Josh, he was immediately whisked into a room and quickly prepared for surgery. With those words spoken, I knew my baby was in God's hands.

When the elevator door opened, there stood Bill in front of the elevator doors like I had never seen him look before. He was standing there with his shirt and pants wet, and with a haunting stare looking back at me. It was at this moment when my whole body began to quiver and shake. As I stared at Bill, I thought, 'Oh! God! No! I cannot lose both of my fellows! For now, I knew as I exited through the elevator door that I was truly entering and walking into the twilight zone.

Bill began to tell me what had happened. He was mowing in the backyard and Josh was riding in his wagon as the neighbor children, Tammy and Tracy were playing with him. Tammy was pulling him around in the yard while Tracey was running along beside the wagon. Then all of a sudden, Josh tumbled out of the wagon in front of the mower! He stated that Josh went under the mower, and at one time he did not even see him. I knew listening to Bill's words, the situation was more than serious, it was highly critical. Bill stated to me as I was staring into his eyes, that he did not know if Josh was alive or not. He said Josh was motionless when he picked him up and brought him to the hospital.

I asked Bill why his shirt and pants were wet. He stated that he did not want me to witness all the blood that had gotten on his clothes. He explained that he had tried to wash as much blood out of his clothes before I arrived. Bill then stated to me through his tears, "At one time, Linda, I never saw him under the mower, I never saw him!"

Bill led me into the waiting room that was located in front of the elevator. The thought came to me: Josh had just turned two years old nine day before. It had seemed for seven years that God had not intended for us to have a family, but then God had opened the door for us to have a family. At that moment I thought, but surely not for only three months. I asked Bill if he had notified our parents. He stated, "No," He then left to phone them. One of the doctors came up to me and asked if Josh had any allergies. I softly replied, "No, no he has no allergies."

The wait began! Bill and I would sit and wait the next four- and-one-half hours before we would see the doctor again. However, within one hour after Bill called our parents, they arrived, along with many of our friends. Actually, our family and our friends practically occupied the whole floor. It was their presence that helped us to endure our nightmare that night. I do not think Bill and I would have been able to live through the whole scenario that was playing out in front of us, without their presence and prayers. For prayers were really being sent tonight!

I would learn later that Bill would not allow Henry to come and get me until Josh was in surgery; he did not want me to witness had Josh looked. This act caused the delay in my knowing, which also meant the accident had happened right after I had left for class! Why? Why? Why did I go to class, began ringing in my head!

I can only remember sitting, staring, waiting, and receiving hugs with words of 'I am so sorry.' I could hear everyone talking, yet, it seemed I was just an outsider listening. I could still feel my body shaking and quivering as I continued to sit. And then, the thought keep creeping up into my mind, my baby is in surgery! And we all prayed and prayed and prayed and prayed!

It was a little before midnight when the doctor returned to call Bill and me back to talk with the doctors who had operated on Josh and to see him before going to Intensive Care. He had had the best doctors around, better than any doctor at St. Thomas in Nashville, Tennessee. Josh's doctors were Bob and Jack, the renowned Ames Brothers. Thank you, Thank you, Lord!

We walked with the doctor through the operating doors into a long corridor. They were wheeling Josh toward us. He looked so tiny and helpless with his head and back all bandaged. I could only stand and stare at him, for they would not allow me to touch him. Only the strength from God kept me from totally collapsing. I knew at that moment I had to be strong for all three of us.

The nurses wheeled Josh onward and exited through the operating doors toward the Intensive Care Unit. I think when I saw his innocent little body all wrapped and bandaged, I became even more numb than ever, or maybe just deeper in shock. I would have many nightmares from this moment onward in my life, and I would suppress these numerous dreams deep, deeper and even deeper each time they occurred.

Doctors Bob and Jack began to describe and explain how serious the situation was and also how extensive the damage was at this time. Dr. Bob stated that each blade of the mower had struck his back and had crushed one rib and had damaged more. He further stated tissue and skin was destroyed and that Josh's body was in shock. I was staring into Dr. Bob's eyes as he stated, "The miracle is that only a fraction closer and the spine would have been in the scenario, but the spine was not damaged in any way. He continued stating how the ribs had been pushed away and had stopped within a fraction of any organ, especially his lungs. I was repeating under my breath, "Thank you, Lord, Oh, Thank you, Lord!"

Dr. Bob continued explaining to us how each process down his spine was struck, but that he had not totally lost any full activity. No vital organ had been damaged from the accident, even though they had come so close, God had been with Josh. He continued onward reporting that Josh did not have all of any processes destroyed, only one or two in a set. I can still remember how I stood there with my body so stiff and yet shaking and quivering. Yes, even more so than any time before listening to him. But then, this nightmare was only in the beginning stages, for time would have to tell us about the tissue. Because of Josh's little body being in shock caused the question in the 'growth of the tissue.'

Josh's head injury had been caused by the frame of the mower and was only minor at this time. Dr. Bob also stated the scapula was broken, but that was the least of his worries for Josh. I could only stare harder into Dr. Bob's eyes as he continued his explanation of all the damage. I was quivering as Dr. Bob stared at me throughout his report. And then! Bill went down, he fainted and fell to the floor! I screamed, "Bill. Oh, Bill," and Dr. Bob stated to all of us, "I was watching and expecting for Linda to faint, not Bill." And, Bill's fainting only pushed me deeper into the depths of this horror.

This night had become the most horrific and haunting night of my life, as well as Bill's life. Our parents stayed with us until Josh came out of surgery to hear how Josh was before returning home, as did some of our friends. However, our best friends, Billy and Connie Hancock, would stay the whole nightly duration. And, we all prayed as hard as we could that night and onward for the tissue to grow and for Josh Wesley Fritz to make it through the night! The doctors had stated to us that they were not sure where they stood with him making it through the night.

The four of us were sitting and talking in the Waiting Room at Jennie Stuart Hospital, when I realized if I had listened to my feelings and stayed home from class, my baby would not be in the Intensive Care Unit. My baby would not have recently been wheeled from intensive surgery over into the Intensive Care Ward. If I had not gone to class tonight, we would all be home and Josh would be in my arms with me rocking him. If I had only stayed home and not gone to class, my baby would not have been in the backyard! And, it was at this time I began to push this nightly nightmare to the back of my memory to only later suppress it deep, deeper, and even deeper within me.

It was shortly after we reached the Waiting Room across from the Intensive Care, I witnessed a nurse pushing a cart with baby diapers and baby bottles to the Intensive Care Unit. I got up from the couch and walked over to the nurse. I stated, "He does not need diapers nor a baby bottle. He is potty trained and he is also weaned." Her answer, "Well, if he gets hungry, he will use a bottle." I stood there shaking as she wheeled the cart inside the Intensive Care Room. Bill came up to me, I just turned around and stated what she had said to me. We could only return to the Waiting Room and wait. The four of us just kept talking and I kept on shaking and quivering.

I was allowed to visit him every two hours for five minutes in the Intensive Care.

As the sun was breaking across the Tuesday morning sky, the nurse from the Intensive Care Unit came and got me. She stated, "Honey, he is awake from his sedation and crying for you. We cannot quieten him.

He needs his mother." I could not run fast enough to that Intensive Care door. Once inside, I rushed to his bedside. I gently picked him up and held him in my arms. His little body was trembling all over, for he was so frighten, so afraid. I sat and held Josh in my arms until his doctors arrived later that morning.

The nurse was so compassionate and kind. She stated it was against the rules for me to be in the Intensive Care Unit, but she felt Josh needed his mother. He had been crying constantly since he woke up. Therefore, I sat in the rocking chair the nurse provided for me holding my baby for the next several hours. He stopped crying and I stopped quivering. And the lady in the bed across from Josh, finally stopped repeating, 'Poor Baby, Poor Baby'.

I stayed with Josh in the Intensive Care Unit until the Ames Brothers arrived later in the morning to check on him. Bill was still sitting out in the Waiting Room with our friends, anticipating the arrival of Drs. Bob and Jack.

When Drs. Bob and Jack arrived, they checked on Josh's performance and vital signs throughout the night. They decided the best decision for Josh would be to move to a private room. Therefore, we were moved immediately from the Intensive Care Unit into a private room on the surgical floor. This arrangement would be our home for the next month, or so. However, we would remain in this first room until Josh outgrew this room, with his toys, toys, and more toys.

The first greatest news, since 6:30 pm the previous night, was when the Ames Brothers examined Josh, and stated, "The tissue had begun to grow!" Thank you, Lord! Oh! Thank you! We had to watch Josh very closely to make sure he did not get on his back. And Bill and I watched him like a hawk!

The first week, Josh laid very still in his bed. He was very content while we read books to him and played what little we could with him. Bill and I took turns watching him very closely at night. I wondered sometimes how we managed with so little sleep. But then, we knew our strength was from God, and the power from all the prayers that was flooding God's throne room.

The news of Josh's accident had spread throughout Hopkinsville and cities and states beyond like wildfire. The hospital started receiving phone calls related to Josh's condition early in the morning. The phone calls would only continue throughout the day and night and into the weeks to come. Many of our relatives living in other cities and states, who had been contacted by our parents, phoned to keep abreast of his progress throughout this nightmare.

Cayce-Yost, a local department store on Main Street, began receiving orders for toys to be delivered to Jennie Stuart Hospital for Josh. We did not know several of the people sending toys, but we knew the majority of the names sending gifts for Josh. Mrs. Gilkey, who ran and worked in the Toy Department, had to start keeping a list of the all toys ordered for Josh in order to stop duplicates being sent. His hospital room became more of a toy department than a room for recovery. Bill brought his toy box to the hospital to keep his toys, but even the toy box became over-flooded with toys.

There was a little boy about Josh's age that was brought to our floor. He was placed in the ward room at the end of the hall. He was all alone, for none of his family ever came to check on him. When I learned of his presence, I would journey down to visit with him when Josh was asleep. The nurses gave me permission to visit with him, to hold him, and to rock him. I took several of Josh's duplicate toys to him to have in his bed to hold and to keep. What a beautiful sweet smile he gave me when he saw the toys. The toys gave him pleasure during the day to play with and to hold while he slept for comfort and security. It was so heart breaking for the nurses and me to witness this little precious boy all alone in a huge hospital room with no-one.

Josh's nurses were some of the most awesome nurses a patient could ever have to take care of their convalescence needs. They became like family to the three of us, and they especially became my comfort and security. Each of them would come to see Josh even during their breaks, and he loved to see them. When he was able to take a bath, he would only allow one of the nurses, Betty, to bathe him.

I stayed with Josh the first weeks, days and nights, without going home. Bill then stated we needed to work out a schedule, for this was going to be a 'long haul' event. I would come early in the morning and stay for Bill to go home and get ready for work. I would go home late at night when he arrived at the hospital after work. He would stay throughout the night with Josh. I would stay until I got Josh to sleep for the night before leaving for home. The first few weeks, friends would stay with Bill throughout the night for comfort. And, what a great comfort they were to Bill for staying. Different friends and family would come during the day to stay with me for company and help if needed. What a blessing each one was to Bill and me giving their time to help us through this ordeal.

It was sometime before Josh was able to return to surgery for a skin graft. We prayed very hard, along with friends, for the first surgical graft to be successful. Bill and I were very apprehensive when Josh was wheeled out of his room and back to surgery. He had already been through so much. Bill and I sat again in the Waiting Room with family and friends for news. Dr. Bob came out and said the surgery went well, now we just had to wait to see if the skin graft was a success.

However, the worse part was every four hours the bandages had to be changed. I can hear his little screams just typing this as they would take the bandages off and applied a new one. He would scream and I would cry. In time, we would learn the graft was an eighty percent take! Okay, twenty percent more, and that meant back to surgery for another skin graft. When will this nightmare end!

Let me insert here just how wonderful Josh's grandfather Fritz was. Dr. Bob told Bill and I about Pop-Pop secretly and quietly asking him to take his skin for the skin graft on Josh, not from the baby. Dr. Bob reported to him that the skin had to come from the patient, not from a donor. I could only cry when I learned what Pop-Pop had offered to do for Josh. What a precious gift he had offered.

In time, Josh returned back to surgery for a second skin graft, only to learn it would be a total loss. I then felt, I cannot stand anymore. Lord, please help me! It had been seven weeks in the hospital and I felt that I was at the end of my rope! But just one look at Josh, my baby, and see that I had to go on 'No Matter What.' But I really knew I could not breakdown now, I had to be strong for my baby and for my husband. And then I thought, what had Daddy always told me throughout my life, "Preserve Linda, always Preserve."

Bill and I took turns going to church Sunday mornings. This particular Sunday, I felt I had gotten a supply of extra strength from God. I knew now I could hold up no matter what happened. I left church knowing that Bill and I were going to be even stronger through this entire ordeal. And besides, one look at Josh, I knew I had the strength to endure whatever it took for my baby.

Josh was progressing greatly, and we were preparing for a third skin graft. I felt very good about this third skin graft. Doctor Bob was allowing us to go home to prepare for the third skin graft. We were elated!

But then, tragedy would strike again. Judy had spent the morning with Josh and me as we waited for Dr. Bob to come to the floor and sign the papers for us to go home. Home for a whole week before the next surgery. I had packed our belongings waiting for the orders to be signed to leave for a week at home.

The morning was passing by quickly, and no Dr. Bob. I would periodically get up from the floor where Josh and I were playing to look out into the hallway to see if he had arrived. Impatient, Oh, yes! For the three of us were going to go home for a whole week. Josh had not seen his home for seven weeks, only the inside of a hospital room. But today, new life seemed to be running through my veins. We were going 'Home' to Southgate, the three of us again.

It was after lunch when I again looked out the hospital room door for Dr. Bob. This time he walked through the entrance door of the Surgical Floor. As I stepped out into the hallway, I heard the crash inside the room. I turned to walk back inside. As I entered the room, there was Josh on the floor bleeding. I let out a scream that brought Dr. Bob and the nurses running. Judy stated he had gotten up this time to follow me and fell breaking his 'glass' baby bottle that cut his hand.

How much more, Lord, how much more? This question ran through my head the rest of the afternoon. How much more? How much more were we to endure?

Doctor Bob picked Josh up and carried him to the small medical office beside the Nurses Station. I followed along with the nurses. Doctor Bob assured me it was not serious, but stitches had to be applied to his little hand. The worse part was Doctor Bob had me to hold him down while he cleaned out the glass, numb and sewed his hand. I tried so hard to hold my tears back, because Josh's little face, was looking up into my eyes pleading, "Help me Mom!" I could only say to Dr. Bob, "I hate you for this, I hate you for making me hold my baby down!" And I cried!

When Doctor Bob finished stitching Josh's hand, I was able to hold him close to me again. However, Doctor Bob stated we needed to stay at the hospital one more night for him to observe Josh after this incident. Then, Doctor Bob placed an adhesive 'Allergic' sign that read 'Allergic Josh Fritz' on his shirt. And he wore that sign all day and all night throughout surgery. Everyone smiled when they read the sign, for everyone in Jennie Stuart Hospital knew Little Josh Fritz.

I called Bill at work to inform him about the accident and the verdict of one more night stay at the hospital. Josh had a hard time resting after we went back to the room for one more night. He sat in my lap for a long time while I just rocked him. I could only say, "Oh, Lord, Please Help us through this afternoon and tonight."

My brother, Howard Stokes, who was an artist, painted a picture of Doctor Bob with the allergic sign with Josh Fritz written on it. I took the painting to Humphrey's Photography, our local photography store located on Sanderson Drive. It is here, I had all of Josh's portraits made and all framing done.

Bill, Josh, and I visited Doctor Bob's office after the painting was framed in order to present the framed painting to him. He, along with his whole staff, were elated to receive the gift. He hung the framed painting in the hallway of his office for everyone to view until the day he retired. After Doctor Bob's death, I asked his children if they would allow me to purchase the painting from them. Their answer was a no. They wished to keep it as one of their treasured momentums of their father. Besides, they stated that the painting was Doctor Bob Ames's favorite treasure.

It was late at night before I finally got Josh to sleep and placed him in the bed. He was sleeping soundly in the bed when the night nurse came in and flipped on all the lights. She was not the regular nurse, matter of fact, I had never seen her the whole time of being in the hospital. I softly and kindly asked her if she could take the vital signs later and not wake him up now. I explained how he had just gone to sleep after such an ordeal. She sharply turned around to me and said in a loud rough voice, "Well, I will have to report your request." And she left the room without turning off the lights.

Thank goodness Josh's regular nurses reported back on duty the next day. They immediately came to Josh's room to check on him and to visit with him, for they were not expecting to see him. One of the nurses reported the rude entry the night nurse had written about my request on not taking his vital signs. We just all had a hardy laugh, because they knew her report was not the way the request was made about taking his vital signs.

I was already packed for our dismissal to leave this morning when Bill arrived. Doctor Bob had signed our dismissal papers and we only had to wait for Bill.

Josh had received so many toys, books, and stuff animals, we had to have two cars in order to go home. The hospital had continued to receive calls in reference to Josh's progress during the whole hospital duration. To our knowledge, Josh had four different denominations of churches praying for him, the Baptist, the Methodist, the Catholic, and the Christian. And people from all walks of life were concerned about our Miracle Child. Bill and I were deeply touched, for it seemed our Little Josh had touched more people in his life than most in their whole life.

We arrived home, and oh, how good it was for the three of us to enter the house again as a full family. Josh immediately took off heading toward his room and Bill unloaded the toys from both cars. When Josh walked inside his room, he went straight to his rocking horse, Cheyenne. I held on to him as he rocked that horse once again, looking up at me and smiling. I looked at him and smiled as I said, "Thank you, Lord!" I have my baby back.

As the time was reaching his bedtime, I started preparing to give Josh a bath in the hall bathroom with the tub. I gathered his soap and shampoo, along with his bath towel. I also gathered a few of his toys to play with and of course, some clean pajamas for him. As I undressed him, he would smile and talk to me, and even laughed. What a great sound to hear resonating through the house, Josh's laughter once again. I helped him in the tub and to sit down on the mat. But when I picked up the soap, my suppressed feelings within me surfaced and I screamed for Bill. I could only run from the bathroom when he entered. I ran to our bedroom and knelt beside my side of the bed and cried, and cried, and cried.

However, that Friday we received news that Granddaddy Cunningham had been killed. He had been showing a friend his hydraulic lift on his tractor, not realizing the tractor was in gear. The bush-hog was hooked up to the tractor, and as the tractor jumped forward, the bush-hog ran over Granddaddy.

Granddaddy and Josh had become great buddies in such a short time. He had wanted to be a great granddaddy, and Josh had made that accomplishment for him. Bill stayed home with Josh, while I attended Granddaddy's funeral. Rest in Peace, Granddaddy!

We returned to the hospital after a week at home for the third and hopefully final skin graft. Josh was prepped again this time for his third skin graft. Again, the whole family was present for this third surgery as they had for the other two. The surgery was a total success! After another week stay in the hospital, we were able to return home to stay. We still had doctor visits to make and 'We' changed the bandages this time. We still had to watch him very closely in order to protect his back. The only question that could not be answered was, would Josh lose any muscular coordination of any kind.

I told Doctor Bob about the bathing incident. He replied, "Linda, you had been in shock all of this time, and you were finally releasing it from within. Time will heal all things." However, I would keep suppressing the nightmare deeper and deeper within for the next forty-nine years.

Time would tell us and even show us if Josh lost any muscular coordination. Josh would demonstrate that he could easily climb on his gym set, run fast, out swim and out swing any of his playmates. Each time I watched him play T-ball baseball I would witness him picking flowers for me in the outfield. He would present them to his 'Mom' when he came to the dugout stating, "I picked these for you." I was the envy of every mother sitting in the bleachers!

He brought such a heartwarming feeling to me. And when he became a power hitter in Little League Baseball by sending that baseball hard to the outfield, and watching him run and jump shooting the ball in basketball, and then becoming one to reckon with in soccer, water skiing, and snow skiing, I knew, by the Grace of God… HE IS OUR MIRACLE CHILD.

Saturday October 4, 1975, we moved into our new home we built in Fairview, Kentucky. We had torn down the 'Old Big House' where Bill and I had begun our married life together. Now, we were back actually where we had begun our life together, but this time as a complete family, for now we had Josh.

Josh enjoying a snack in his high chair

Tuesday September 2, 1975, Josh had turned four years old. He was growing up too fast. Now, he was helping us to move into the new house where we settled in and continued our lives together. This would be the house Bill and I would live in the rest of our lives, and with many great memories with Josh Wesley Fritz included.

A few months after moving in, another panic moment occurred with Josh. On this particular morning, we arose with heavy rain, for a storm had rolled in the night before, and was continuing with heavy rain throughout the day. Josh had not been feeling well for the past few days. We had taken him to see Dr. Howard, Josh's Pediatrician, a few days before. He had examined him and had prescribed some medicine. However, this particular afternoon, Josh crawled up on my lap for me to rock and comfort him in the late afternoon. I rocked and sung to him for the next few hours, when all of a sudden, his whole body went totally limp. Just at this time, Bill arrived home and was opening the door. As he entered, I screamed for him. He rushed to us rocking in the chair. I stated, "He has gone limp, Bill. He is Totally limp! Oh, God!"

I wrapped a blanket around Josh as we rushed out of the house. The three of us crawled into the car, and Bill sped out of the driveway onto the road toward Dr. Howard's office in Hopkinsville, Kentucky. The rain was pouring, no beating down upon the car as we drove onward toward Dr. Howard's office. 'Help' was all I could repeat.

As I tightly hugged onto Josh, I prayed the hardest I could, asking the Lord to please heal my child and not allow anything bad to happen to him. Again, I went to the Lord asking as hard as I could, "Please, not another incident of possibly losing my child again, Lord. No! No! Not again! Please, save and heal my baby! Please! Please!"

Bill was as scared as I was, he would glance over at us and ask, "How is he?" I could only softly say, "Please hurry!" It was hard for him to drive, because the visibility was bad enough with this hard rain, and then with the wind blowing fiercely. Here we were, another bad scare with our baby, with our son, Josh.

When we arrived, Dr. Howard was waiting for us. He checked Josh over and kept him to observe for a while before we were able to take him home. He then prescribed some medicine for Josh to take for the next few days. Dr. Howard assured Bill and me that Josh would be fine and would be up running through the house in a few days. Hallelujah! Thank you, Lord.

No one truly knows how much stress or scare you can withstand in your life, not until you have experienced that stress or that scare. You have to face it head-on; that is your only real choice. I thought I had experienced all I could handle with the first incident, however, I guess this round made me even a stronger person.

Josh 4 years old

Josh's first Christmas was a total joy for Bill and me, as well as our families. Josh was the first grandchild and first great grandchild in my family, as well as the first nephew and great nephew. The only thing Josh would say he wanted for Christmas was 'Bubble Gum!' Even to Santa Claus, Josh would tell him that he wanted 'Bubble Gum!' Therefore, his big stocking was filled with bubble gum on Christmas Day morning Tuesday, December 25, 1973.

Josh grew up into a handsome young man. During his childhood he learned to water ski, play T-ball, Little League Baseball as a power hitter, and soccer being a player to reckon with. He joined the Cub Scouts, with his mom, as the Den Mother. He would continue on by joining the Boy Scouts and being the youngest Scout in Kentucky to earn the Eagle Scout Award. He graduated from high school, and would later marry. He presented us with two handsome grandsons, one grandson would present us with a great grandson.

Josh Christmas on his inchworm

Josh has and still works hard providing a great living and life for his family. He is a pure blessing sent from Heaven Above.

LAST WORDS: I truly do not know how anybody can live their life without the Lord Jesus Christ, for He is the comforter, the infallible Savior, the loving Savior, omnipotent, and so much more. I was presented with dreams beginning my fourth year in school of a beautiful little boy, and these dreams followed me until the day I was presented with that little boy, Josh Wesley Fritz.

It took me over 49 years to be able to speak about this tragedy and to even write the words down trying to describe that haunting tragedy. I was only able to write a few sentences at a time before crying and having to cease my story, for I had buried this tragedy so deeply within me. I do believe I have now written all of the story I suppressed, because I can now breathe better than ever before. I feel a huge weight has now been lifted from me. I can now, somewhat, accept the tragedy, however, I still cannot forgive myself for attending class that fateful night after having so many feelings and thoughts telling me to skip class that night. However, I probably will not forgive myself to my dying days.

This tragedy did cause me to become a better prayer warrior. Josh is probably the most prayed over person that I know. He had so many real prayer warriors praying and lifting him up to the Lord that fateful night, in addition to the days and months that followed.

Throughout my childhood life and my life beginning with Bill, I had prayed for this child, and following that Monday September 10, 1973, I do believe I became much like a prayer warrior. From the day we received Josh, I prayed thanking God for him and lifting him back up to God to hold in His hands throughout his life. The fear of losing Josh has followed me the rest of my life.

I would pray to God so hard each time Josh left the house to go to camp, on a date, and later when he would have to travel by a vehicle or an airplane to a job in another state, to return home safely. He and his vehicle had more protective arms around them each time he traveled, as did the airplane each time he flew. I would ask God to send not only protective hands around the plane, but also for the pilot, for I was in contact with God asking for 'Special Forces' to surround that plane to bring him home safely. I also prayed and worried when he was a teenager and left for work or with his friends.

There was that time when Bill and I arrived home one Saturday night from eating out with our friends, when Josh stated he and his friend was going to ride up to the Dairy Dip in Elkton, Kentucky. I simply stated okay and be careful. As Josh and his friend walked out the door toward Josh's car, I quietly talked to God asking Him for special protective arms around the boys and the car. A short time later, Josh and his friend was brought to our house with injuries!

Josh had been run off the highway by two vehicles racing down Highway 68 and coming straight at him. Josh had hardly any room on his side of the highway to go! The car in his lane was traveling at high-speed hitting Josh's car and sending the car and the boys across the road landing out in a field. They were able to climb out of the car and make it to the highway in hope someone would stop to help. And someone did stop and help. You see, cell phones had not been invented at this time for Josh to have in order to call home.

The lady offered to take the boys to the hospital, and they certainly took her up on the offer. However, as they approached the house, Josh told her to stop because his mother would take him to the hospital, and she stopped. Again, we were witnessing as Josh and his friend entered into the house with their injuries, another time that Josh could have been taken from us. The young man called his dad to report the accident. We took Josh to the emergency room to have him checked over and to mend his injuries.

Bill had the car towed to our driveway. He then covered the car with a tarpaulin so no-one would see the car before we had contacted our family. The father of the young boy with Josh in the wreck that night, came to check on Josh. He and I were looking at the wreck when a car pulled in the driveway with some of Josh's friends who had come to visit. I walked them into the house to see Josh and talked a short time before returning outside.

When I returned outside, a car was driving out of our driveway. At that moment, he stated, "Oh! That was the car that ran the boys off the road last night!" I ran down the driveway to see the license plate, but the car had sped off too fast. He told me they stopped and asked if that was the car in the wreck last night, and also if anyone had been injured. No-one knew about that wreck except the five of us.

Again, God answered my prayers for my precious son, Josh Wesley Fritz.

With all My Love,
Mom

Five Generations. Great Great Grandmother Robbbie Cunningham holding Destin Kirche Fritz, Great Grandmother Dolly Stokes, Grandmother Linda Fritz, Dad Josh Fritz

Printed in the USA
CPSIA information can be obtained
at www.ICGtesting.com
LVHW062332190124
769097LV00019B/422